To Kenneth From Gran
Starcevich 1986

Nn Oo Pp

Qq Rr Ss

Tt Uu Vv

Ww Xx

Yy Zz

The Sharon
Picture
Dictionary

The Sharon picture dictionary

by
Frank Daniel
and
Evelyne Johnson

Sharon Publications, Inc.
Cresskill, N.J. 07626

All correspondence and inquiries should be directed to Sales Dept., Sharon Publications, Inc., 105 Union Avenue, Cresskill, New Jersey 07626.

Sharon Publications Inc. is an Edrei Communications Company.

Cover Designed by Rod Gonzalez

ISBN #0-89531-032-5

Printed in Singapore by Khai Wah Litho Pte Ltd.

accident
A thing that happens by mistake

actor
A person who takes a part in a play or movie

add
To put things together

adult
Grown up, like your parents

address
The place where one lives

Mr. T. Bear
15 log Way
Grizzlytown
Bearsville

afternoon
The time of day between noon and evening

age
How old a person or thing is

air

What we breathe.
It is all around us

airplane

A machine that
flies through the air

airport

A place where
airplanes take off and land

alike

Things that are nearly the same

aloud

Something
that can be heard

alley

A narrow street
between buildings

animal

Any living thing
that is not a plant

alphabet

All the letters
we write with

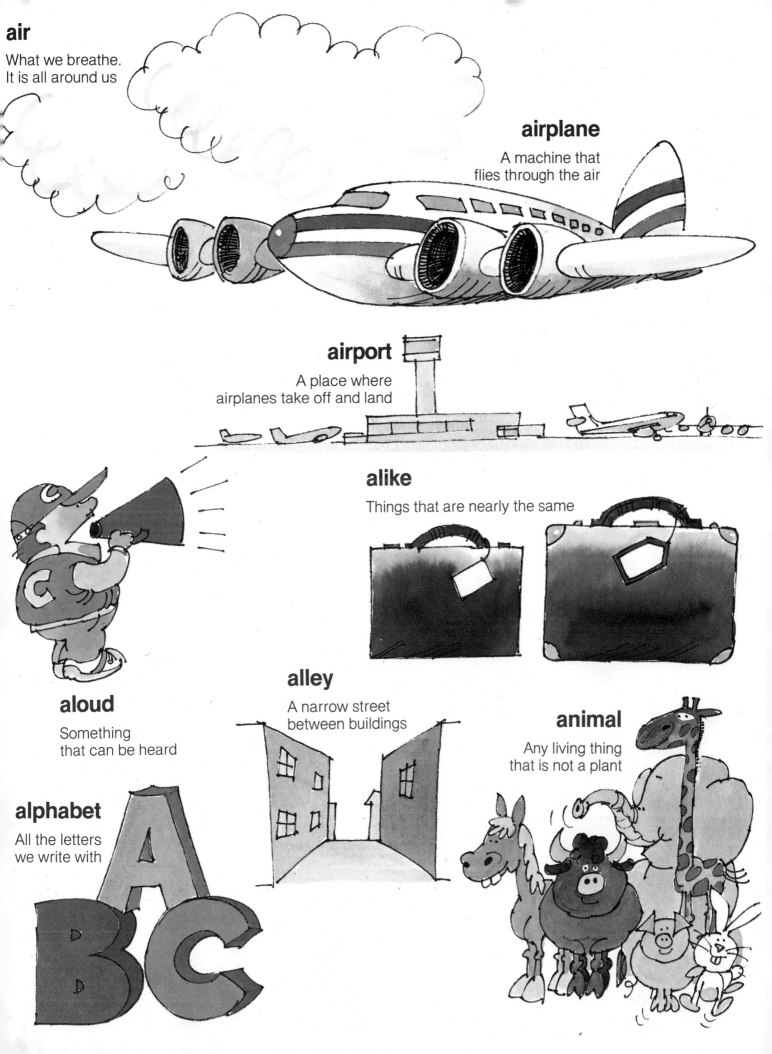

ankle

The joint between
the foot and the leg

apart

Away from

appliance

A small machine
for a particular use

arrow

A slender stick with
a point to be shot from a bow

art

A drawing,
painting or
sculpture

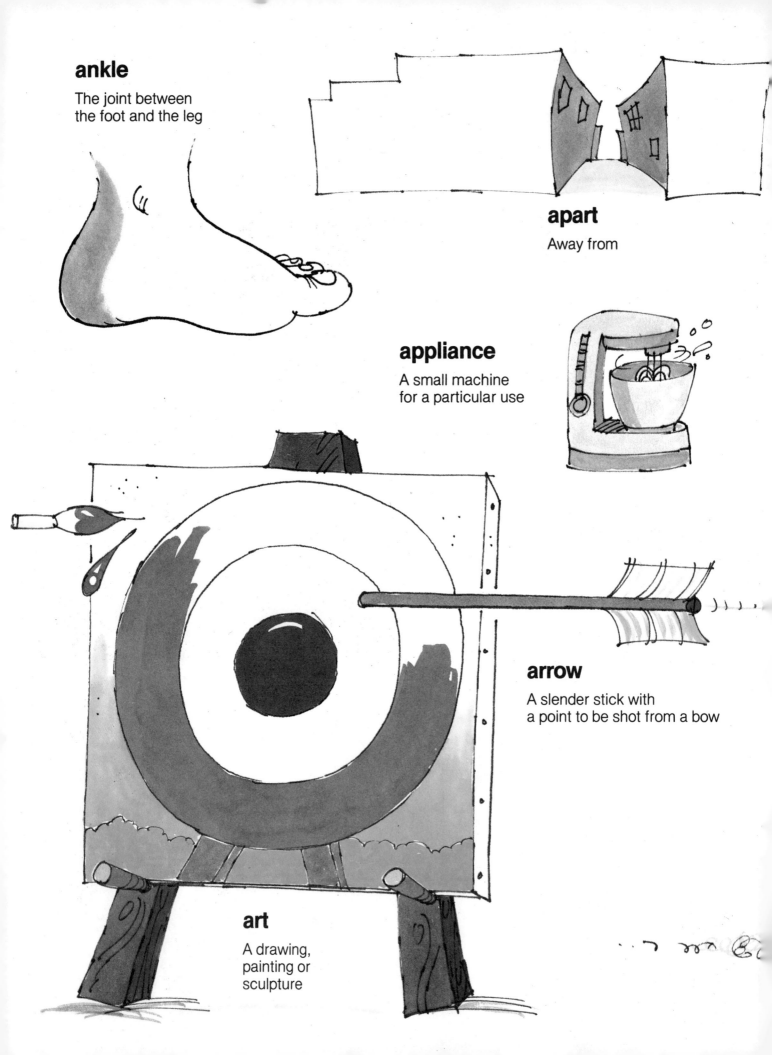

astronaut

A pilot or
passenger on a
space ship

author

A person who writes
books or articles

artist

A person with
a special skill
in art or music

auto

A car
with a motor

awake

Not asleep

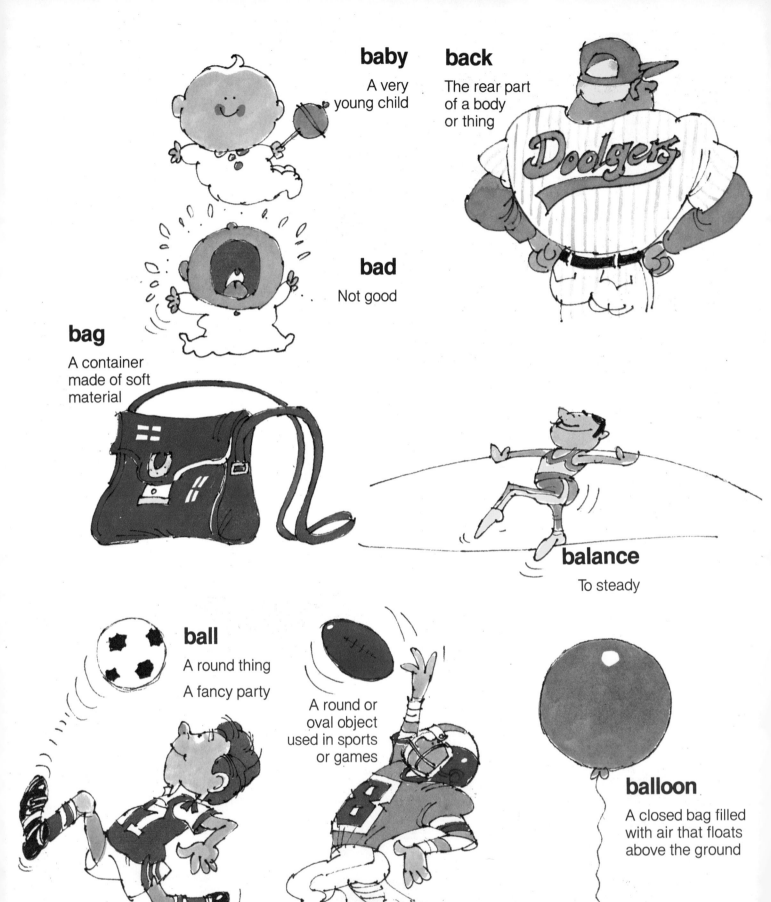

baby
A very young child

back
The rear part of a body or thing

bad
Not good

bag
A container made of soft material

balance
To steady

ball
A round thing
A fancy party

A round or oval object used in sports or games

balloon
A closed bag filled with air that floats above the ground

bake

To cook with dry heat in an oven

bakery
A place where cookies, bread, cakes and other baked goods are made or sold

band
A group of people who play music together

bandage
A strip of cloth used to cover injuries

bank

A building or a container where money is kept

barber

A person who gives haircuts

barn
A farm building used to keep animals and their food

basket
A woven container

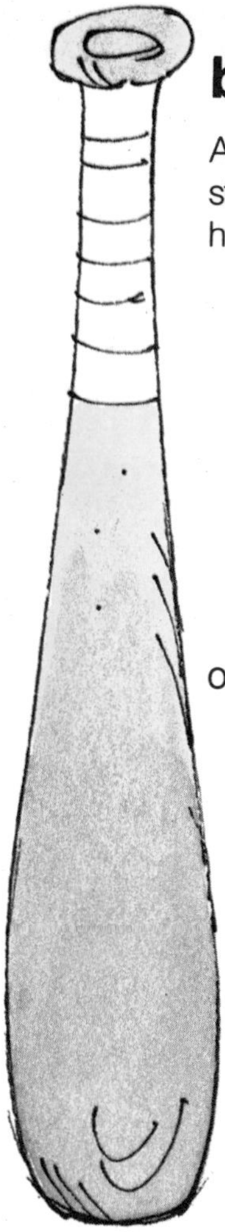

bat

A wooden stick for hitting balls

A small furry animal that flies at night

bath

To wash the body in water

beach

A sandy shore of a body of water

bed

A piece of furniture to rest or sleep on

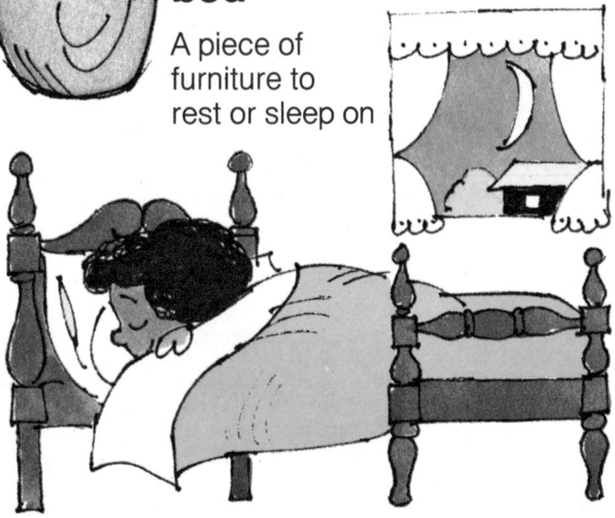

before

Earlier

behind

At the back of

bicycle

A vehicle with two wheels and pedals to make it move

big
Large

boot
A covering for
the foot and leg

booth A small section closed off
for telephoning or voting
or in a restaurant for eating

bridge A structure built over water or
railroad obstacles so people can
go from one side to another

caboose The last car of a freight train

cage A space with wire or bars on the sides

calendar a chart to show days, months and year

OCT.

can

Know how to, have the ability to

A metal container

camera A machine for taking photographs

CAT

cap A head covering with a small brim in front

A cover for a jar or bottle

COUNT DRACULA

card

A piece of heavy paper

cape

A point of land going into the sea

A sleeveless garment that hangs over the shoulders and arms and back

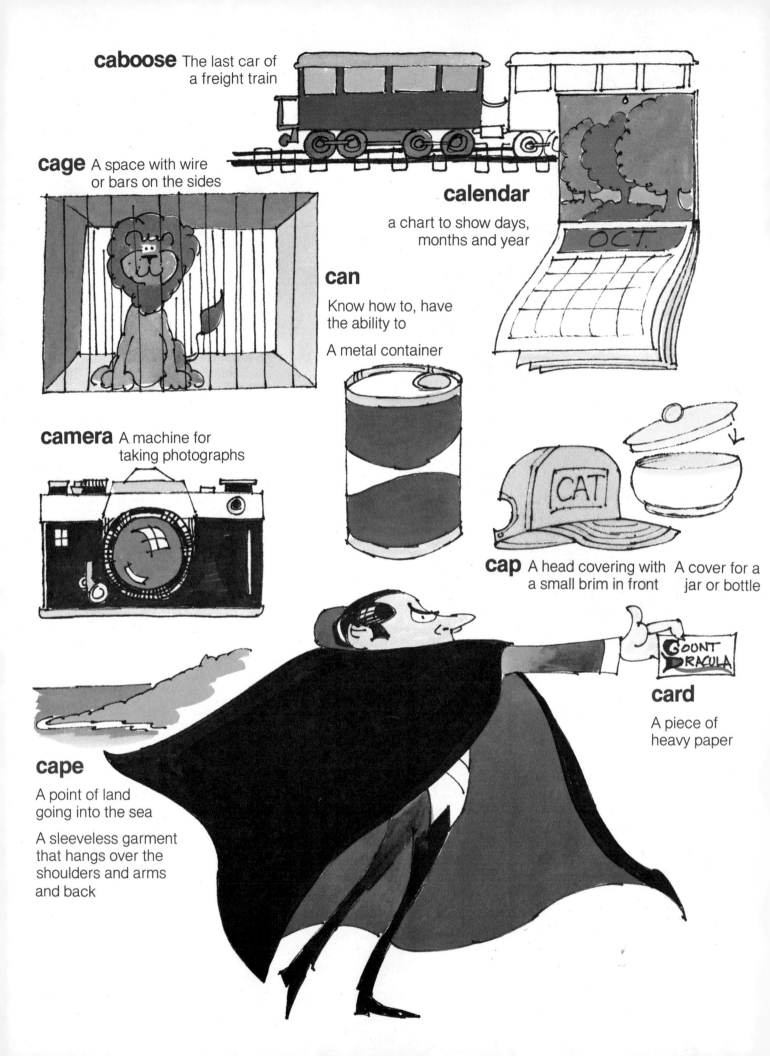

carpenter A person who builds things from wood

carriage Posture

A vehicle with wheels to carry people or things

cave

A hollow space in the earth with an opening to the outside

center

The middle

cereal

The seed from wheat, oats, corn or rice

chest a large box for storing or shipping

chair

A piece of furniture on which a person sits

The upper front part of the body

child

A person who is not grown up

chore

Light work to do around the home or farm

chorus A large group of singers or a part of a song

choose To pick

circle

A ring that is perfectly round

clown An actor who wears funny make-up and clothes at the circus to make you laugh

clock

An instrument for measuring or telling time

coat

A piece of clothing with sleeves that is worn over other clothing

A covering of a surface such as paint

collect

To bring things together in one place

coo

A perso who prepare food fo eatir

cooperate To work together

cousin A child of an uncle or aunt

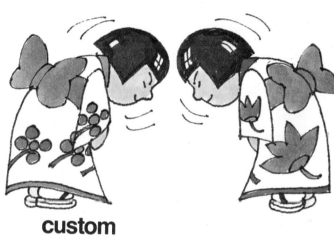

custom

The passing down of customs from generation to generation

cover

Something to put over another thing such as a lid or top

cushion

A soft pillow to rest on

crowd A large number of people gathered together

dab

A small amount

To touch lightly

dairy

A place where butter, cheese and other milk products are made

A store where milk products are sold

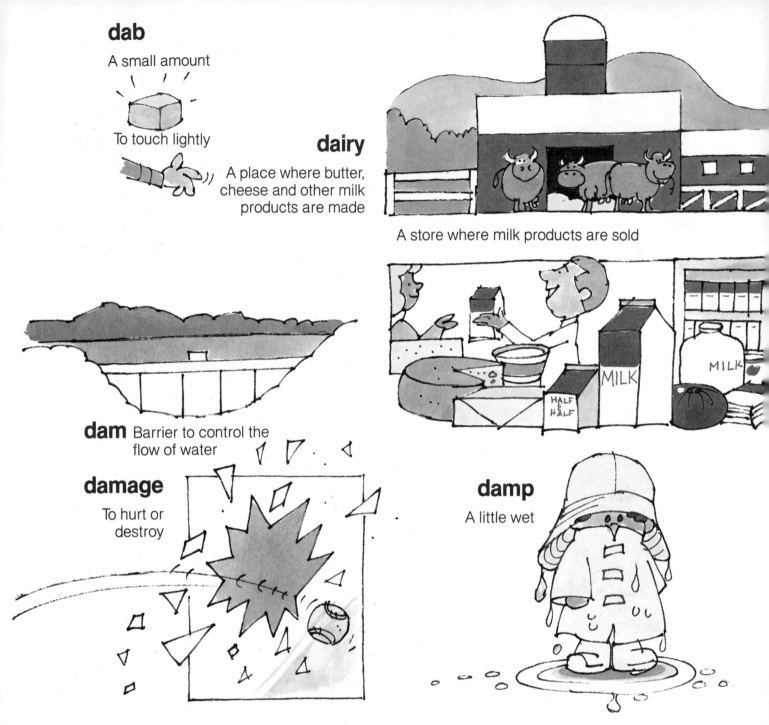

dam Barrier to control the flow of water

damage

To hurt or destroy

damp

A little wet

daughter A female child

dance

A series of movements to music

dawn The time of day when the sun comes up and it gets light

deaf

Having poor
or no hearing

deft

quick and
skillful

dent

A hollow or
bend made in
a surface by
a blow

delicious

Very pleasing
and good to eat

dentist

Doctor who
treats and takes
care of teeth

depot A railroad or bus station

BUS DEPOT

derrick

A large machine
for lifting
heavy objects

A tower on top
an oil well
to support
the equipment

depth

How far down
something goes

descend

To go or come down

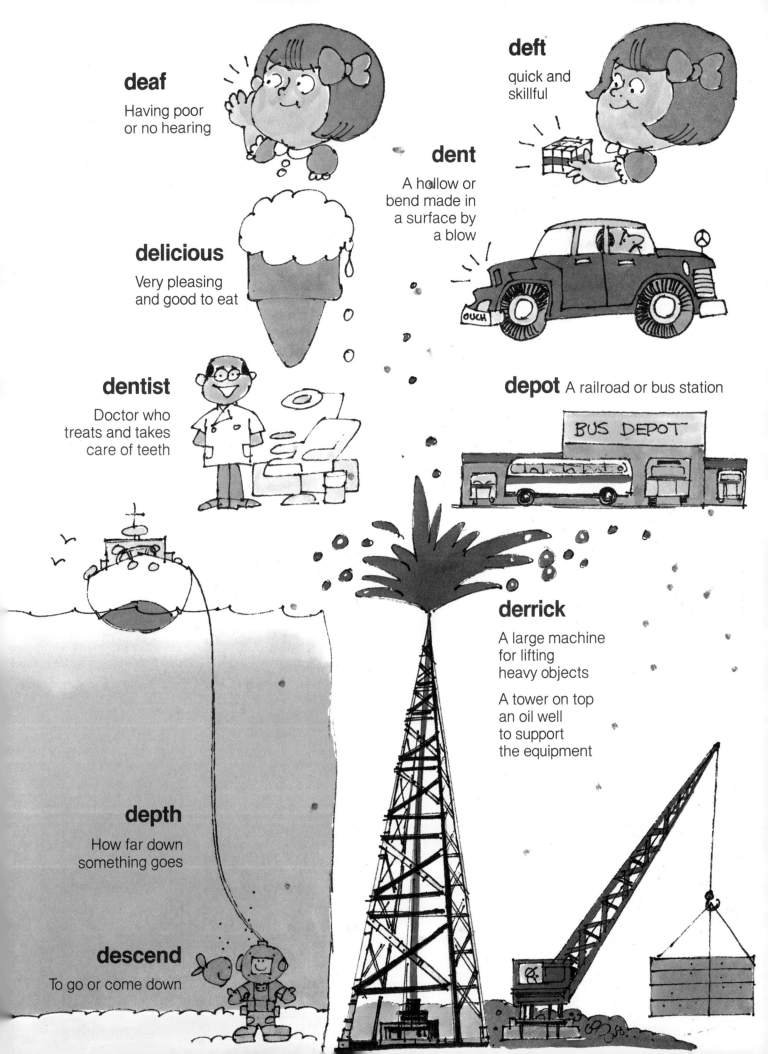

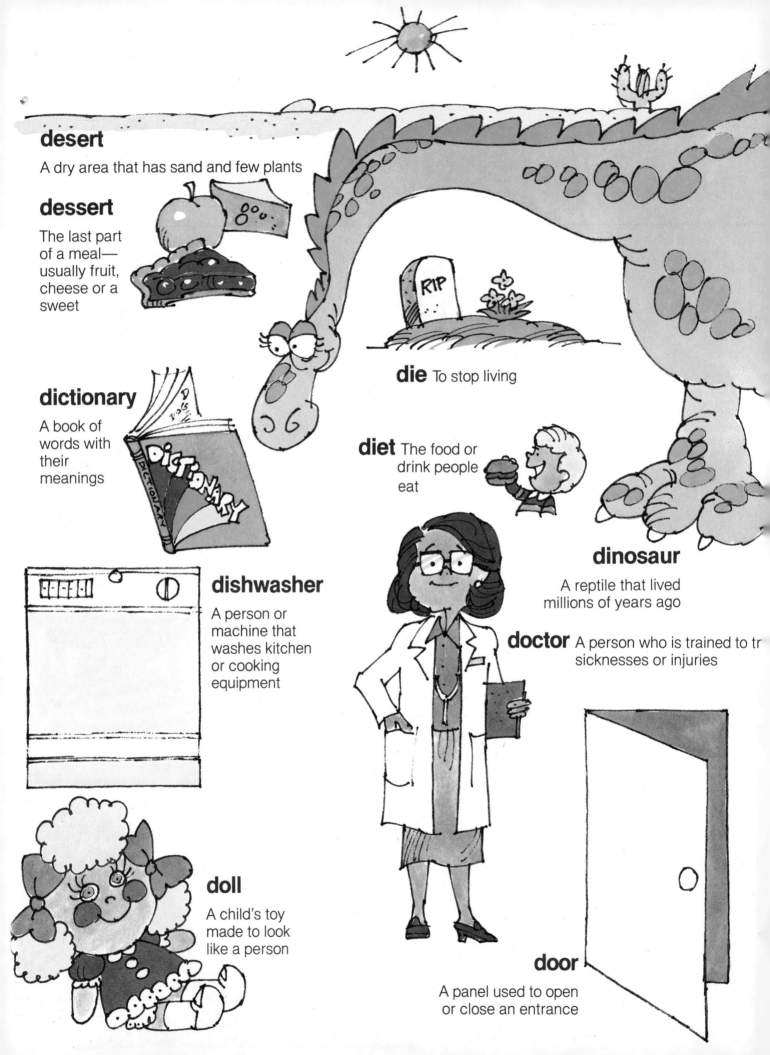

desert

A dry area that has sand and few plants

dessert

The last part of a meal— usually fruit, cheese or a sweet

dictionary

A book of words with their meanings

dishwasher

A person or machine that washes kitchen or cooking equipment

doll

A child's toy made to look like a person

die To stop living

diet The food or drink people eat

dinosaur

A reptile that lived millions of years ago

doctor A person who is trained to tr sicknesses or injuries

door

A panel used to open or close an entrance

dozen A group of twelve

drawer A box that slides in and out of furniture

drink To swallow liquid

drowsy Ready to fall asleep

dwarf A very small person, animal or plant

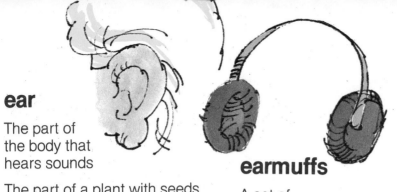

ear

The part of the body that hears sounds

The part of a plant with seeds

earmuffs

A set of coverings for the ears

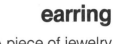
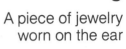

earring

A piece of jewelry worn on the ear

earth The world we live in

eat To take food or meals

eavesdrop

To listen secretly to other people talking

echo

To send back or repeat a sound

HEY!

HEY!

HEY!

edible

Safe for eating

elbow

The joint between the upper and lower arm

A curved metal band to join pipes

elect To choose by vote

ELECT
EMORY

elevate

To raise up

embrace

To hold in the arms or hug

emerge

To come out

embroider

To decorate with stitches of color

To make up extra details (as a story)

engine

A machine that makes power to make other machines work

engineer

A person who makes engines go

enter
To come in

entire Whole thing

$\frac{1}{2}$
$\frac{1}{4}$ $\frac{1}{4}$

entrance Door or place to go in and out

envelope A paper holder to use for mailing or keeping

equal
Exactly the same

erase
To make something disappear by rubbing

etiquette
Rules that tell how to behave

$+\frac{1}{1}\overline{3}$

error
A mistake

erect
To build or cause something to stand up

evade
To avoid or escape

evening
The end of
day or beginning of night

ever Always

evil Wrong or wicked

examine
To look at
carefully

exercise
Physical or
mental activity

exit
A way or door
to get out of
a place, going
from a place

eye The part of the
body used for seeing

expensive High priced

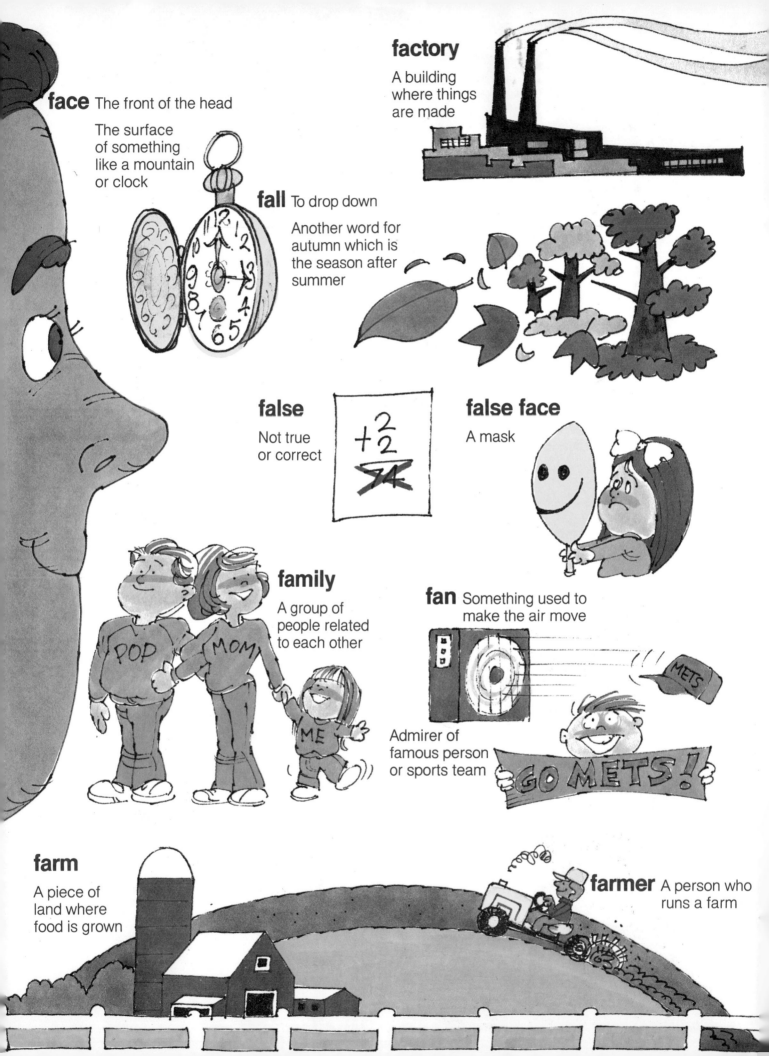

face The front of the head

The surface of something like a mountain or clock

factory A building where things are made

fall To drop down

Another word for autumn which is the season after summer

false Not true or correct

false face A mask

family A group of people related to each other

fan Something used to make the air move

Admirer of famous person or sports team

GO METS!

farm A piece of land where food is grown

farmer A person who runs a farm

fasten To attach or close

feel To touch

father The man parent

female A woman, a girl

fence A barrier to keep things in or out, usually made of wood or wire

ferry A boat used to carry people and goods across water

few A small number

finger One of the five body parts that extend from the hand

fingernail The hard covering at the end of the finger

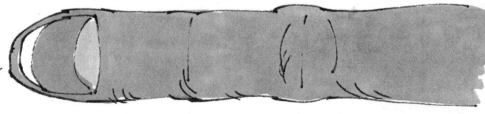

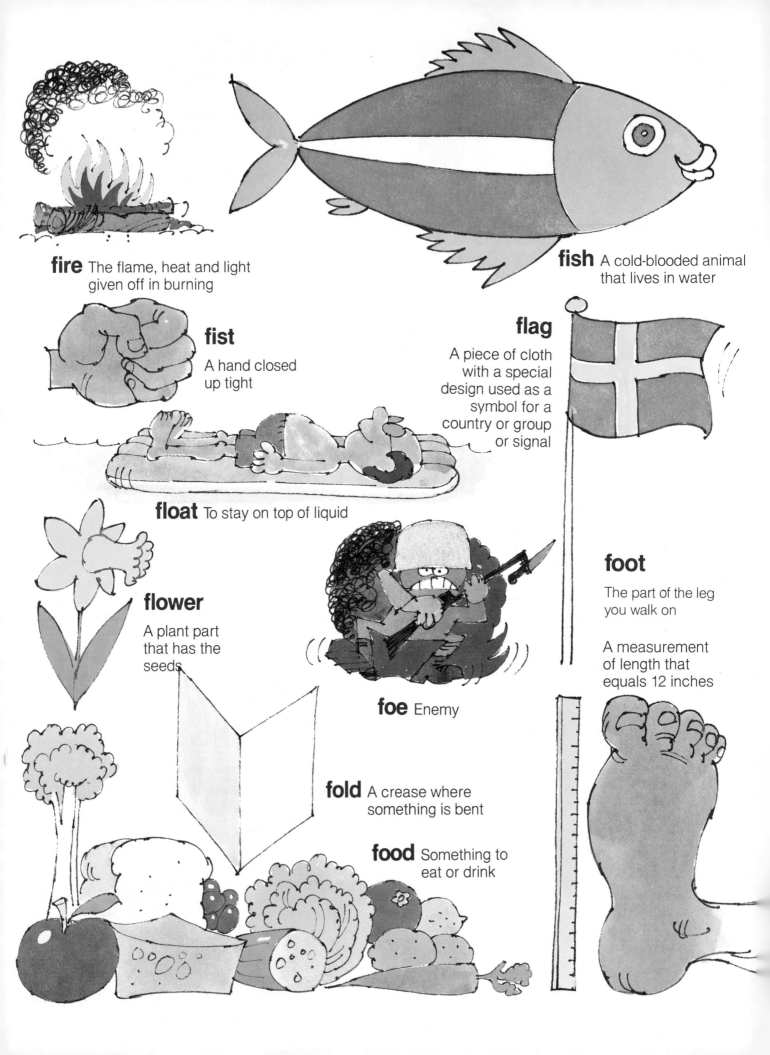

fire The flame, heat and light given off in burning

fish A cold-blooded animal that lives in water

fist A hand closed up tight

flag A piece of cloth with a special design used as a symbol for a country or group or signal

float To stay on top of liquid

flower A plant part that has the seeds

foe Enemy

foot The part of the leg you walk on

A measurement of length that equals 12 inches

fold A crease where something is bent

food Something to eat or drink

forearm The part of the arm between the hand and the elbow

forehead The part of the face above the eyes

fork

A place where something splits into 2 or more directions

A tool for picking up food

friend

Someone to like and trust

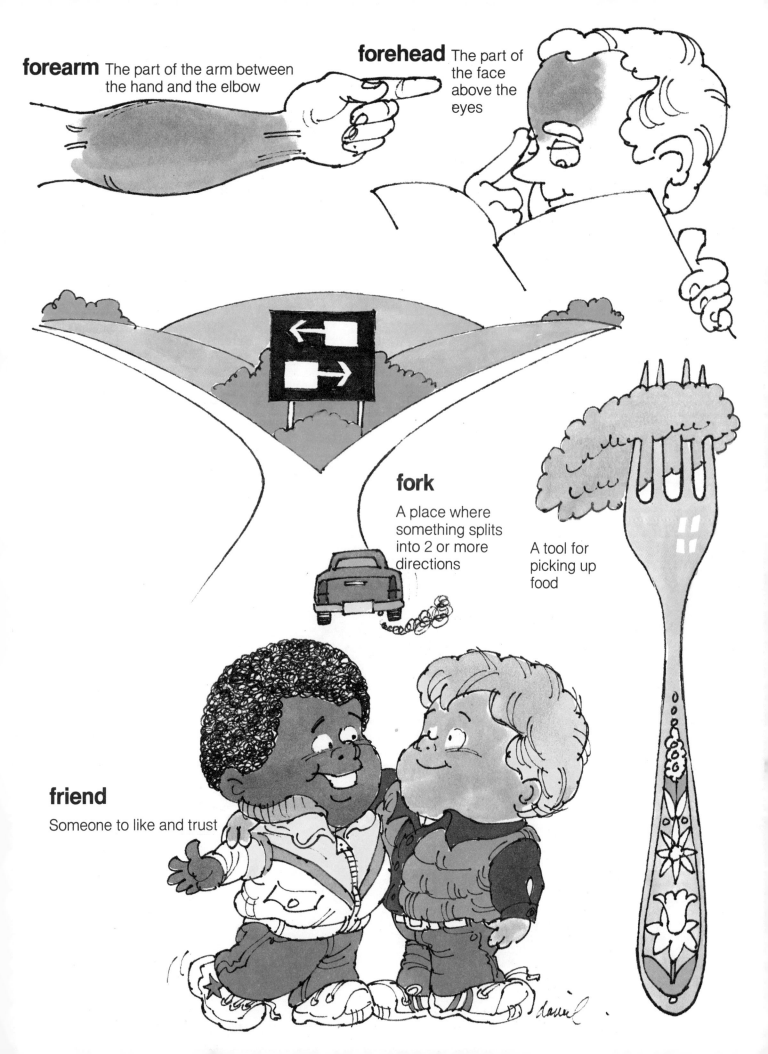

game
A way of playing

gang A group or people who do things together

garage A place where cars are kept or serviced

garden A piece of ground where flowers or vegetables are grown

garment
A piece of clothing

gate
A part of a fence that opens and closes

gather

To bring together

giant

Something or someone that is very large

gift

A present

glass

A material you can see through that breaks easily

A container made of glass for drinking

glove

A cover for hands, for keeping hands warm in winter

girl

A female child

glue
Something that makes things stick together

grade A class in school

The slope in a road

grandfather
The father of person's mother or father

grandmother
The mother of person's mother or father

granddaughter

grandson

grate
Rub against sharp metal to cut into bits

greeting
A message of good wishes

HAPPY BIRTH DAY

grin
A big smile

grocery
A store where food is sold

grouch
A person who sulks and complains

grownup
Someone who has finished growing
An adult

group
A collection of people or things

guest
Someone who comes to visit

guide
To show the way

EXIT

gush
To pour out suddenly

WELCOME

gym A place where people exercise or play games

hair
Thin fine strands that grow on the skin

hammock
A swinging bed hung in the air between 2 poles

hamper
To get in the way

A container with a cover for storage

hand
The part of the body at the end of the arm

handbag
A small bag or case that is carried

handle
The part of an object that is made to be held

hang
To fasten something from above

hangar
A shed to keep airplanes in

hanger
An object to hang clothes on

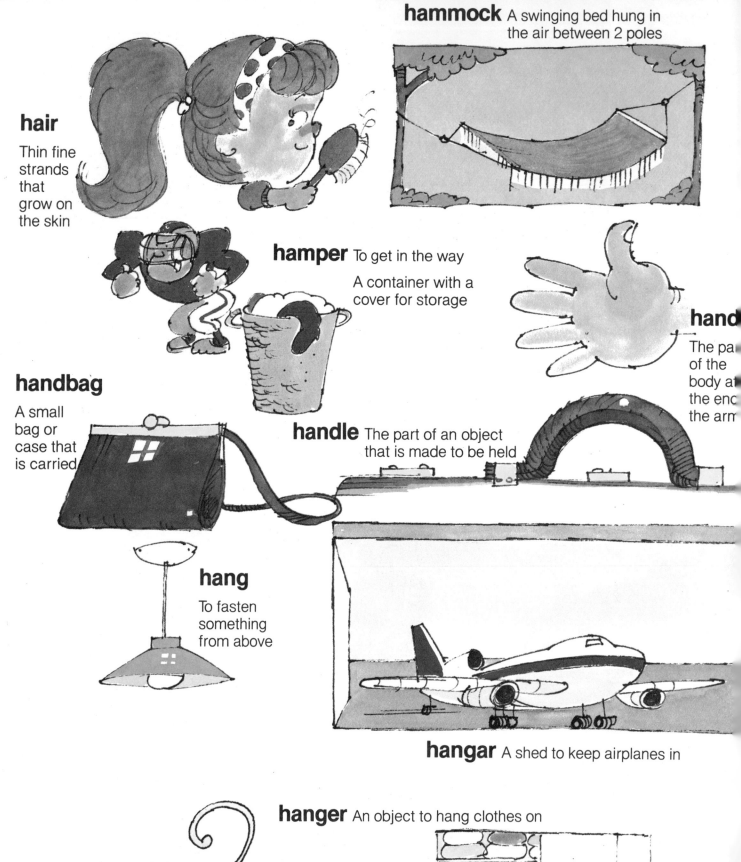
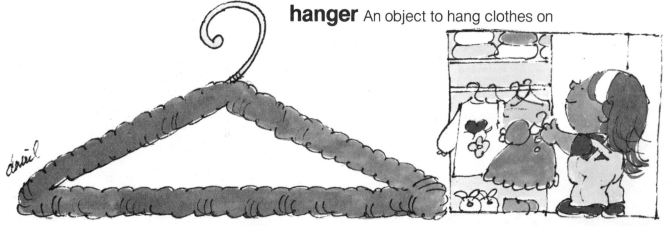

harm
Injury or hurt

hat
A covering to wear on the head

hatchet
A small ax

hay
Dried grass to be used as food for animals

heap A pile of things

head
The part of the body that has the ears, eyes, nose and mouth

heat Warmth

heart
The part or the body that pumps blood

heel
The back part of the boot below the ankle

height
How high something is

helicopter
An aircraft with propellers on top

help To assist

herd A group of animals

hermit
A person who lives alone

hide To keep out of sight

The skin of an animal

hole

An empty place

hook

A curved object that is used to hold, catch or fasten something

hot

Very warm

hospital

A place where doctors care for sick or injured people

SUN VALLEY HOSPITAL

EMERGENCY

house

A building in which people live

hotel

A building where people pay to sleep in a room

HOTEL

huge

Very large

husband

A married man

HAPPY BIRTHDAY TO MY HUSBAND

MR. & MRS J. DOE

ice Frozen water

ice cream

A frozen dessert made from cream, sugar and flavorings

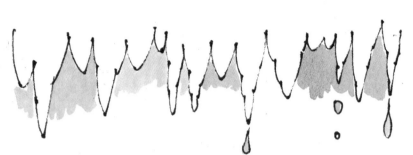

icicle A pointed piece of ice formed by drippings

idea

A thought formed in the mind

idle

Not busy

identical Exactly alike

Igloo An eskimo's house

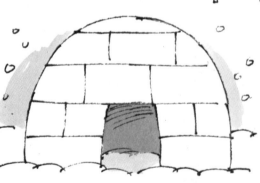

ill Not healthy or well

illustration

A picture used to explain or duplicate

imitate

To copy or behave like another person

DRAWING OF A MAN WITH A TALK BALLOON.

immediately Right away

incorrect

Not right
or proper

incline

A slope or slant

ink

A colored liquid
used for writing

infant

A baby

inn

A small hotel

insert

To put in

injure

Harm or
damage

inside

the side that is in

instruct To teach

TO TEACH

interior

The inside part

interrupt

To stop a person talking or acting

invalid

A person who is sick or injured

invention

Something made or thought up for the first time

INVENTORS DO IT FIRST

HI!

invert

To turn upside down

invitation

To request the presence of someone at an event or plac

invisible

Not able to be seen

BIRTHDAY PARTY!

& YOU'RE INVITED!

joke Something said or done to make people laugh

jolly Full of fun, cheerful and happy

journalist A person whose job is writing for a newspaper or magazine

jot To make a quick short note

joyful Feeling happy and gay

juggler A performer who juggles balls or other things

juice The liquid from fruits, vegetables or meat

jumble To mix things together in confusion

jump

To spring off the ground using the legs

jumper

Someone or something that jumps

A dress without sleeves

junk

Trash. Useless things that are ready to be thrown away

jungle
Area that has a great many vines, trees and bushes

juvenile

Young. Not yet an adult

kayak

A small pointed Eskimo boat covered on top except for a hole in the middle for a person to sit

keel
A strong beam that runs down the center of the bottom of a ship or boat

keen

Having a sharp cutting edge or point

kennel

A shelter for dogs

kerchief

A square scarf around the head or neck

kettle

A cooking pot with a cover

key
A shaped piece of metal that is used to open a lock

keyboard
A row of keys on a piano, typewriter or computer

keyhole

The hole in the lock to put in the key

kick

To hit with the foot

kid
A baby goat or child

kidney A part of the body that filters out waste

kill To put an end to

kilt A knee-length pleated skirt worn by men in Scotland

kin All the relatives in a family

kimono A loose gown with long wide sleeves and tied with a wide belt worn by men and women in Japan

kindergarten A school or class for children before first grade

king The male ruler of a country

kiss To touch the lips to show affection

kite A light wooden-framed toy that is flown in the air on the end of a string

kitchen A room where food is prepared

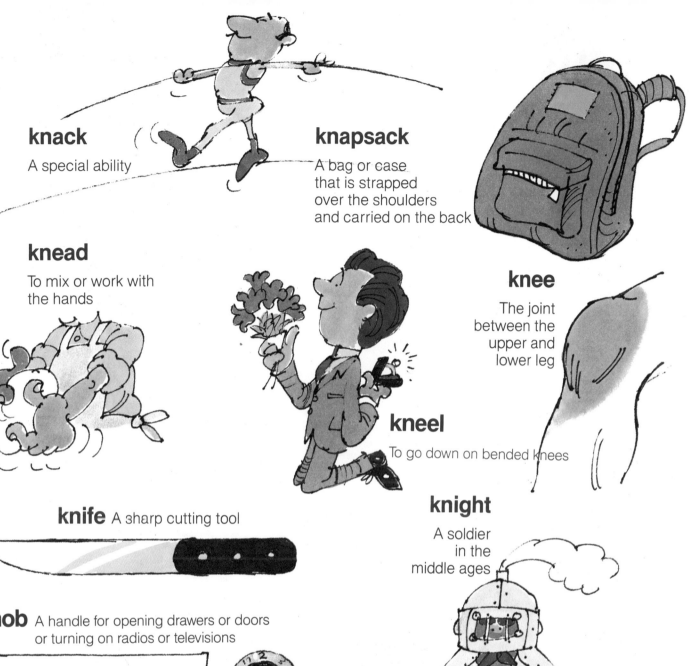

knack

A special ability

knapsack

A bag or case that is strapped over the shoulders and carried on the back

knead

To mix or work with the hands

kneel

To go down on bended knees

knee

The joint between the upper and lower leg

knife A sharp cutting tool

knob A handle for opening drawers or doors or turning on radios or televisions

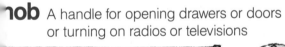

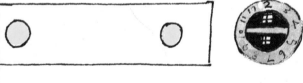

knot A fastening made by tying together pieces of string or cord

knuckle

One of the joints of the hand

knight

A soldier in the middle ages

label
Anything put
on something
to identify it

FRAGILE

ladder

A thing used for climbing
up and down with two sides
connected by rungs

ladle A spoon with a long handle
and large bowl

lake An inland body of water

lamp

A device that
gives off light

land Earth not covered by water

language

Speech either
spoken or
written

lantern

A container
for holding
a light that
can be carried

lap

The front part of a sitting person from the waist to the knees

laugh

To make sounds that show amusement

laundry

A room where clothes are washed

lazy

Not willing to work

leader

A person who goes ahead or shows how to do something

lean

To rest on a slant

leave

To go away

left The remainder

leg One of the lower limbs of the human body

The parts on which furniture stand

inchworm

length How long a thing is

letter One of the parts of the alphabet

A written message

THANKS MOM!

level Having a flat surface

library A place where books are kept

lick To touch something with the tongue

lie Something a person says that is not true

NO.. I, DIDN'T THROW A BALL.

lift To raise up

light A form of energy that makes it possible to see

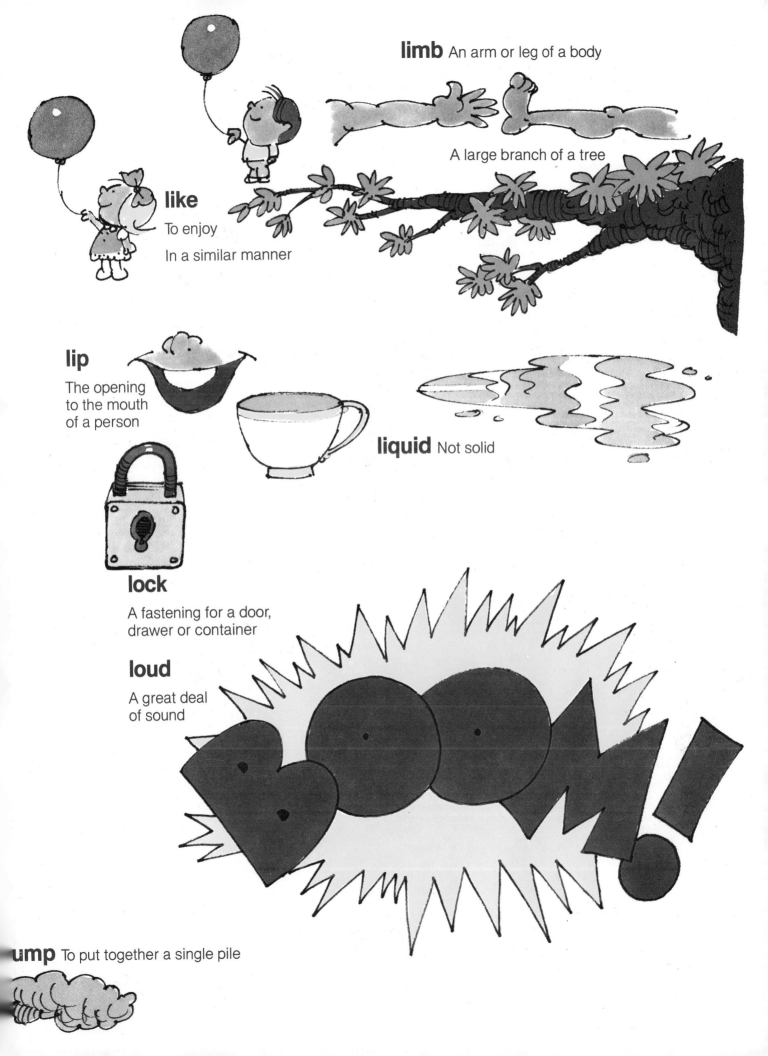

limb An arm or leg of a body

A large branch of a tree

like

To enjoy

In a similar manner

lip

The opening to the mouth of a person

liquid Not solid

lock

A fastening for a door, drawer or container

loud

A great deal of sound

ump To put together a single pile

machinery A device with moving parts that does things faster than people

magazine A printed collection of stories and pictures that comes out regularly

magnet A piece of stone or metal that attracts iron or steel

magician A person who performs magic tricks and illusions

magnify To make something larger

mailman A person who carries and delivers letters and packages through the postal system

majority More than half

mallet A wooden hammer

male Boy or man

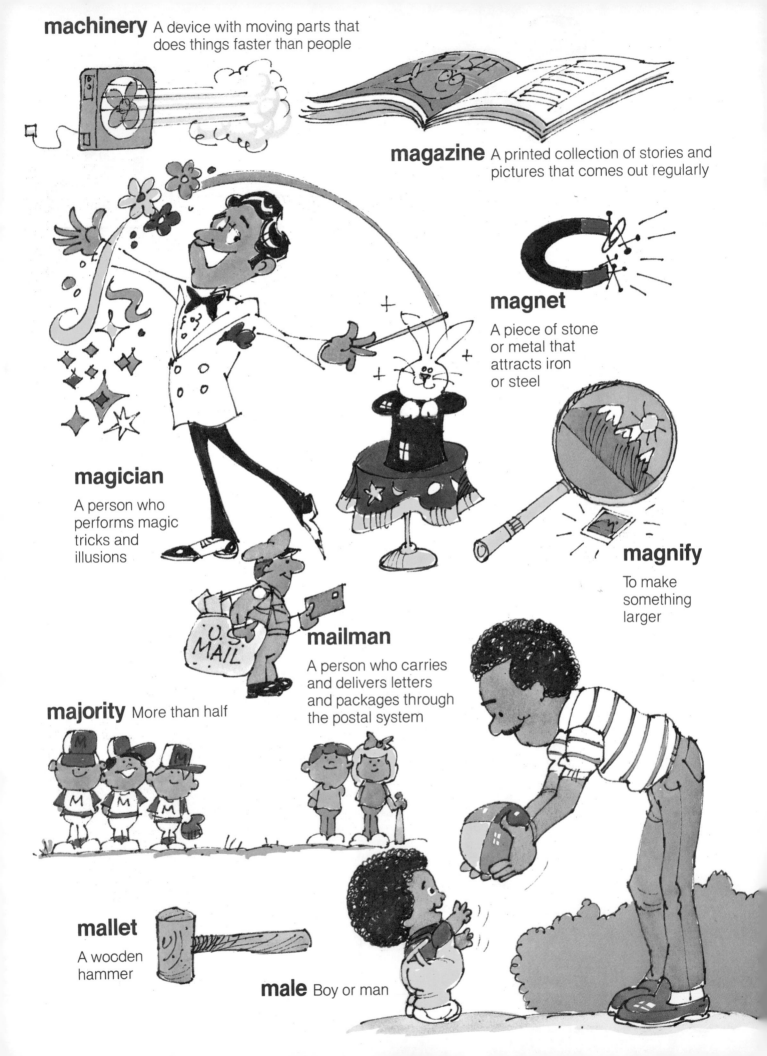

mammal Animals that have fur, warm blood and feed their young with milk

man
Adult male

mane
The long hair that that grows on the head of horses and male lions

manger
A large box from which horses and cows eat

manicure
Cleaning, shaping and polishing of fingernails

map
A drawing that shows where place are

mansion
A very large beautiful house

marionette
A puppet or doll with strings that make it move

marry
To become husband and wife

mascot
Something to bring good luck

mask
A covering to hide the face or make it look different

match
To put things together that are similar

A piece of wood or cardboard that makes a flame when scratched

mattress A pad to sleep on

maze A complicated arrangement of paths

meal The food eaten at one time

medal A badge given as an outstanding act

mechanic
A person who makes or repairs machinery

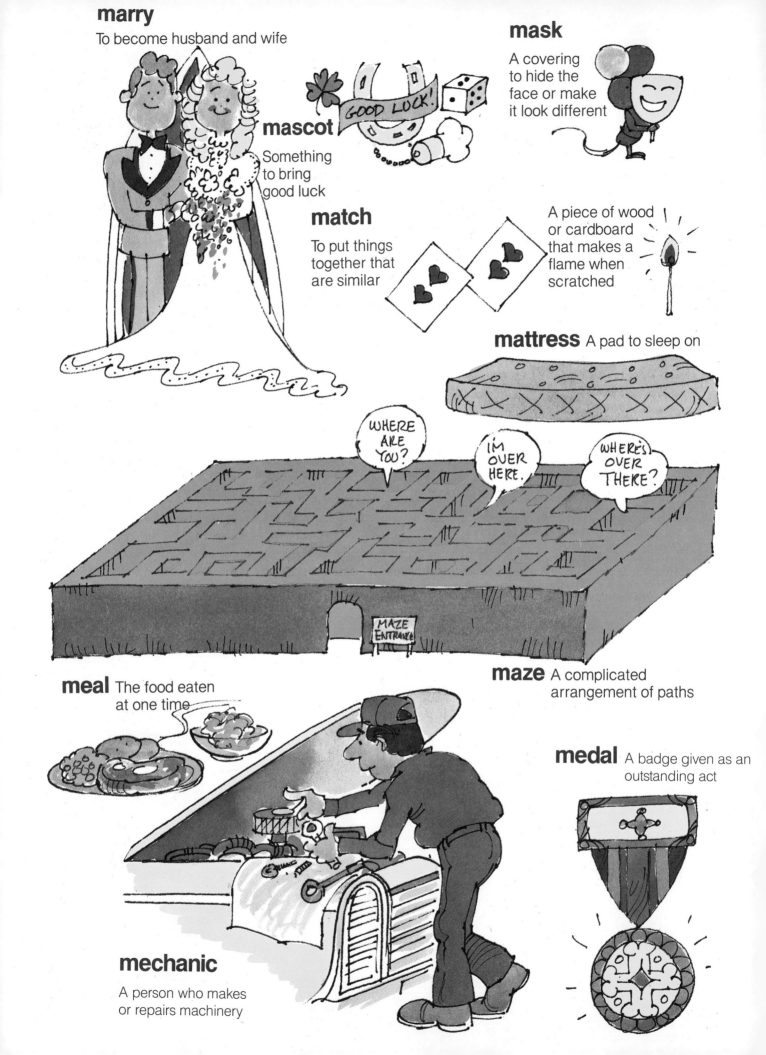

medicine Something used to treat or prevent sickness or pain

melt
To become liquid

memo
A short note or letter

mend To fix or repair

middle
The center

midget
A very small person or thing

mirror
Something that reflects a picture or image

mistake
An error

mitten A covering for the hand with one part for the thumb and the other part for other 4 fingers

mixer Machine that combines ingredients into a mixture

mob

A large group of people

model A person or thing that is a good example of something to be copied

SPITFIRE 1ST

mop A stick with a sponge or yarn on one end that is used for cleaning purposes

morning The first part of the day

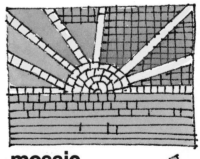

mosaic

A picture or design made by putting together small pieces of colored material

mother

A woman who has a child or children

motor

A machine that makes other machines work

mouth
The part of the body through which a person or animal eats

muff

A soft tube made of cloth or fur to keep hands warm

mug
A heavy drinking cup with a handle

movie
A motion picture

nail A thin piece of metal hammered into things to hold them together

The hard covering at the ends of fingers and toes

nap A short sleep

napkin A piece of cloth or paper used to wipe hands and mouth while eating

narrow Not wide

ROAD NARROWS AHEAD

neat Clean and tidy

neck The part of the body that joins the head and shoulders

nephew A son of a person's brother or or sister

FROM UNCLE FRED

HAPPY BIRTH-DAY

nest The home of a bird

new Something just made

newborn Just born

newscast

A radio or television program that tells what is happening

nibble

To eat or bite quickly

nick A cut or notch

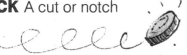

niece

A daughter of a person's brother or sister

night

The time between sunset and sunrise

nip A small sharp bite

noise Loud sounds

nose The part of the face above the mouth used for breathing and smelling

note

A short written message

A musical tone

nudge

A light push

nurse

Someone trained to take care of people who are sick

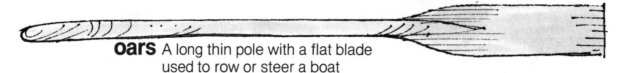

oars A long thin pole with a flat blade used to row or steer a boat

object

A thing that can be seen and touched

oblong A shape longer than it is wide

observe

To watch closely

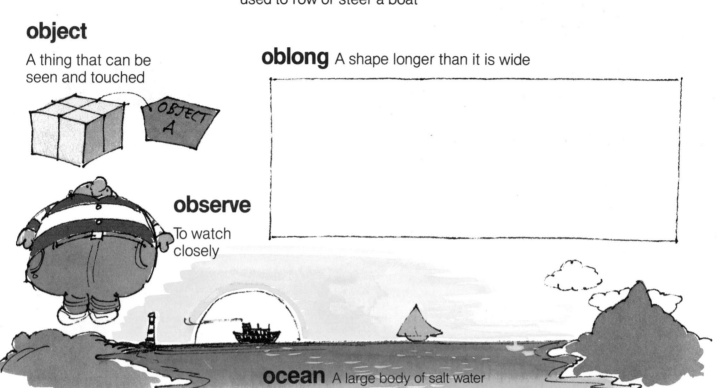

ocean A large body of salt water separating land areas

occupation The work a person does to earn a living

occupy

To take up time or space

odd

Different or unusual

odor Smell

office A place where the work of a business is done

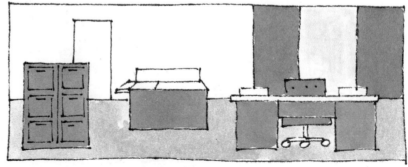

often Many times

old Having lived or existed a long time

omit To leave out

once One time

open Not shut

opposite

A differing view or opinion — Some thing or some place on the other side

orchard A place where fruit trees are grown

oral Spoken not written

orchestra A group of musicians who make music together

The ground floor of a theater

origin
The beginning of something

outing A trip for pleasure

outline
A brief description

oval Having the shape of an egg

oven
An enclosed place used for baking

over On top or above

overcast Covered with clouds

overhear
To hear something accidentally

overcoat
A heavy outdoor coat

overshoes
Rubber of plastic shoes or boots worn over other shoes to keep them dry

pack A group of similar things, animals or people

To put into a container

pad A cushion or piece of thick material

page One side of a sheet of paper

pail A round container with a flat bottom and a handle used for carrying things

pain An ache or hurt

paint A mixture of colors with liquid used to cover or coat other objects

To cover something with color or colors

SHARON PAINTING CO.

painter A person who paints pictures or things

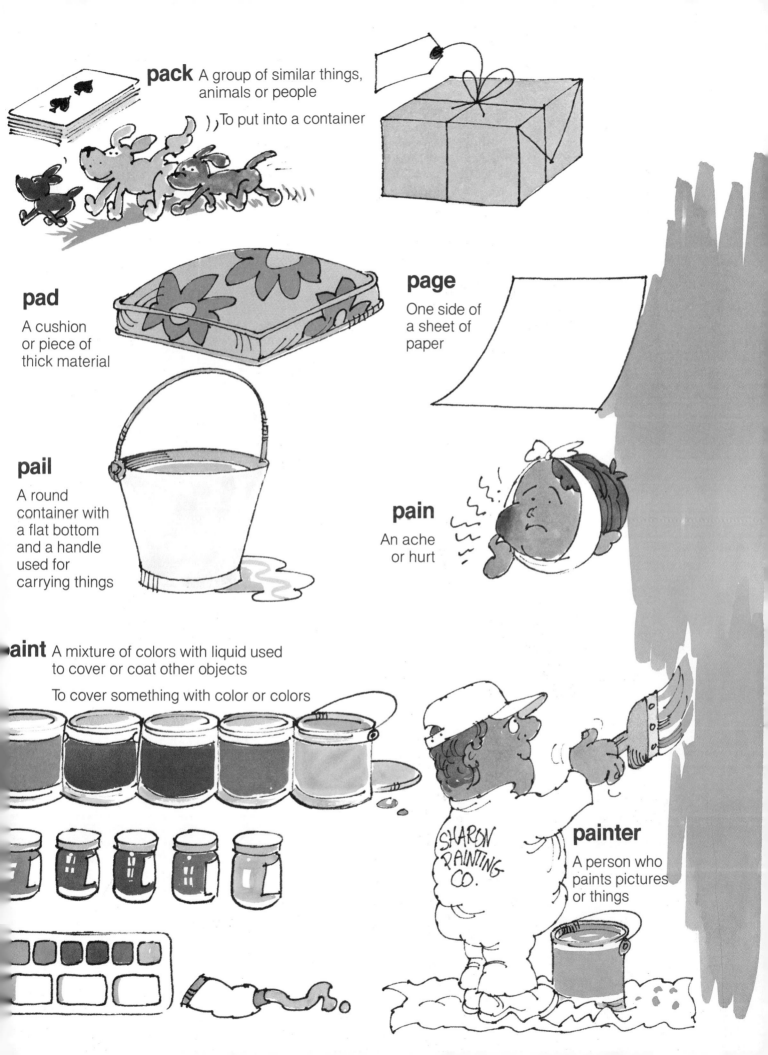

pair
Two of anything similar in form

pajamas A shirt and pants set usually used for sleeping

palette
A thin board that artists use to mix their paints on

palm
The inside of a persons hand

A type of tree that grows in warm climates

pan
A dish used for cooking or baking

pancake A flat thin cake cooked on a pan or griddle

pane A sheet of glass in a window or door

pants Trousers

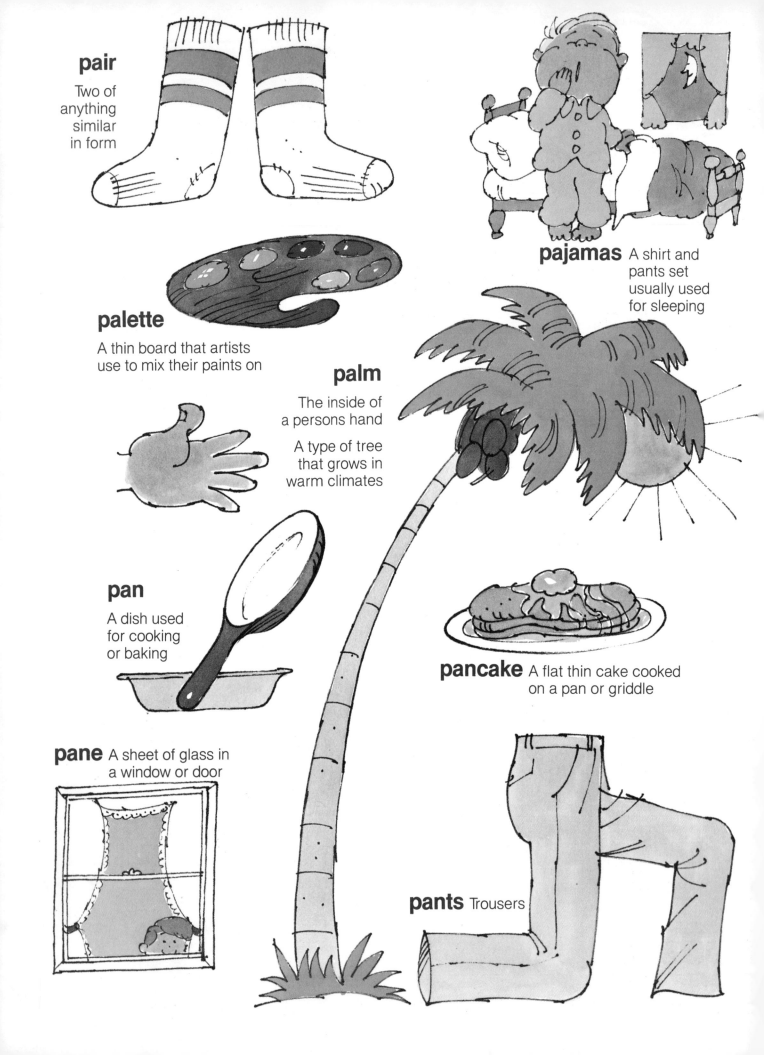

parade A public event where vehicles, musicians or bands pass before people

parent A father or mother

part Not the whole thing

party

A gathering of people for fun, pleasure or purpose

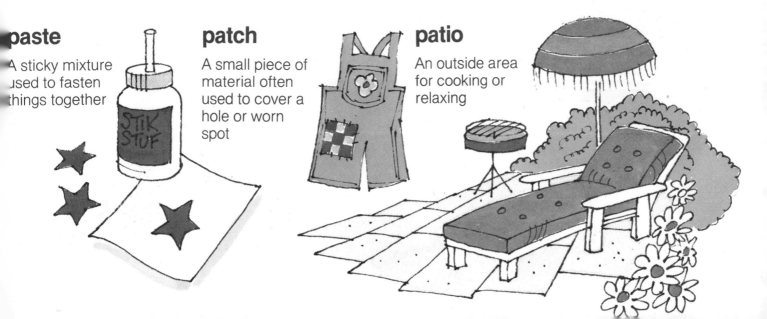

paste

A sticky mixture used to fasten things together

patch

A small piece of material often used to cover a hole or worn spot

patio

An outside area for cooking or relaxing

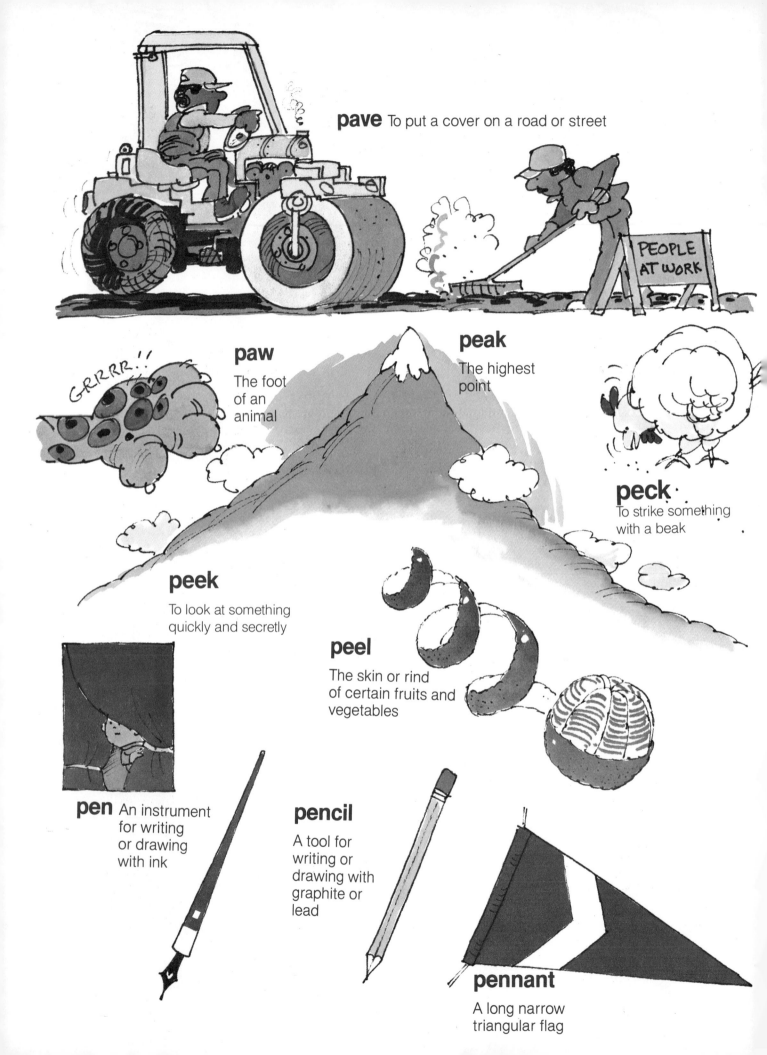

pave To put a cover on a road or street

paw The foot of an animal

peak The highest point

peck To strike something with a beak

peek To look at something quickly and secretly

peel The skin or rind of certain fruits and vegetables

pen An instrument for writing or drawing with ink

pencil A tool for writing or drawing with graphite or lead

pennant A long narrow triangular flag

people
Men, women and children

pet
To stroke or pat gently

An animal kept for fun

petal
A part of a flower

photograph
A picture taken with a camera

me and matt

picnic
A meal eaten outdoors

pin
A thin piece of wire used to attach things together

piece
A thing that is part of something

pinch
To squeeze between the thumb and fingers or between other surfaces

pole
A long thin rod or wood or metal

pond
A small lake

pine
An evergreen tree that has leaves like needles or cones

pot A container for cooking; or growing plants

puddle

A small pool of water

puppy A young dog

push

To press against something to move it

To shove

puzzle Something that is difficult to do or solve

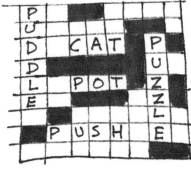

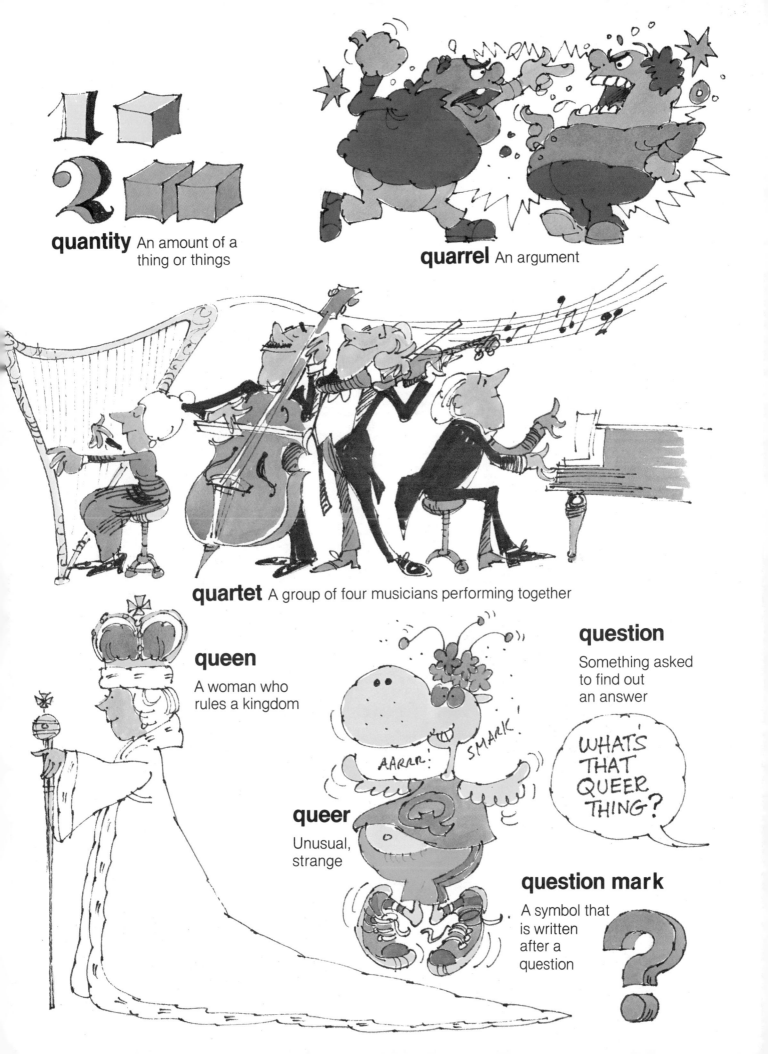

quantity An amount of a thing or things

quarrel An argument

quartet A group of four musicians performing together

queen

A woman who rules a kingdom

queer

Unusual, strange

question

Something asked to find out an answer

question mark

A symbol that is written after a question

quick Fast

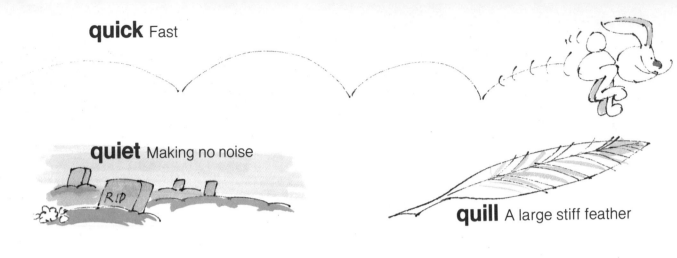

quiet Making no noise

quill A large stiff feather

quintet A group of five musicians performing together

quit To stop doing something

quiz
A short test

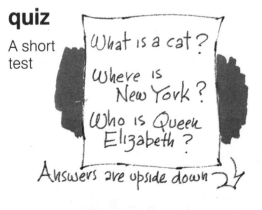

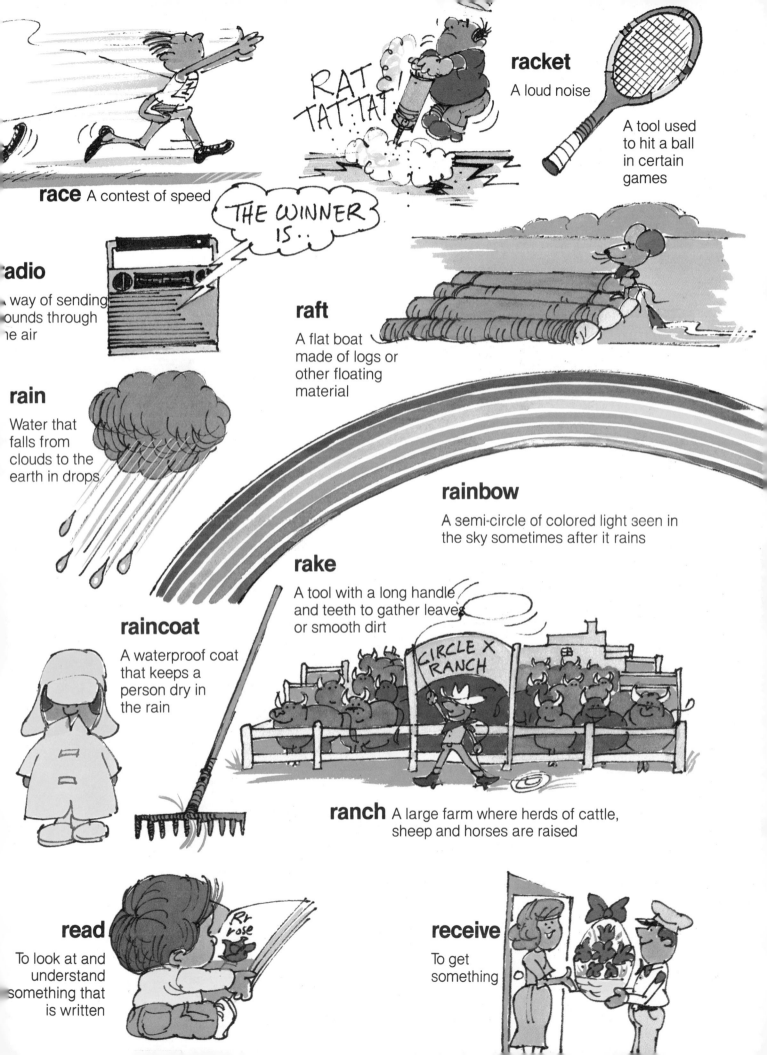

race A contest of speed

racket A loud noise

RAT TAT TAT

racket A tool used to hit a ball in certain games

radio A way of sending sounds through the air

THE WINNER IS...

raft A flat boat made of logs or other floating material

rain Water that falls from clouds to the earth in drops

rainbow A semi-circle of colored light seen in the sky sometimes after it rains

rake A tool with a long handle and teeth to gather leaves or smooth dirt

raincoat A waterproof coat that keeps a person dry in the rain

CIRCLE X RANCH

ranch A large farm where herds of cattle, sheep and horses are raised

read To look at and understand something that is written

Rr rose

receive To get something

recipe

Directions for preparing food

record

To make a copy of something

To keep an accurate account of something

rectangle

A four-sided shape with 2 sides longer than the other two

reel

A spool on which something is wound

refreshment

Food and drink

refrigerator A box that is kept cold so food will not spoil

regret

To feel sorry about something

restaurant A place where people can go to buy and eat meals

rhyme

A story or tale with the last word of each sentence having a similar sound

riddle

A question that is hard to answer

rifle A gun with a long barrel

BANG!

rim

The border or edge of something

ring

A noise made by a bell

A piece of jewelry worn on a finger

robot A machine that can do somethings like a person

POLISH MOP RUB

ON OFF

rock

A stone

To move back and forth

round

A shape like a ball or a circle

ruler

A person who rules

A flat strip to measure or draw straight lines

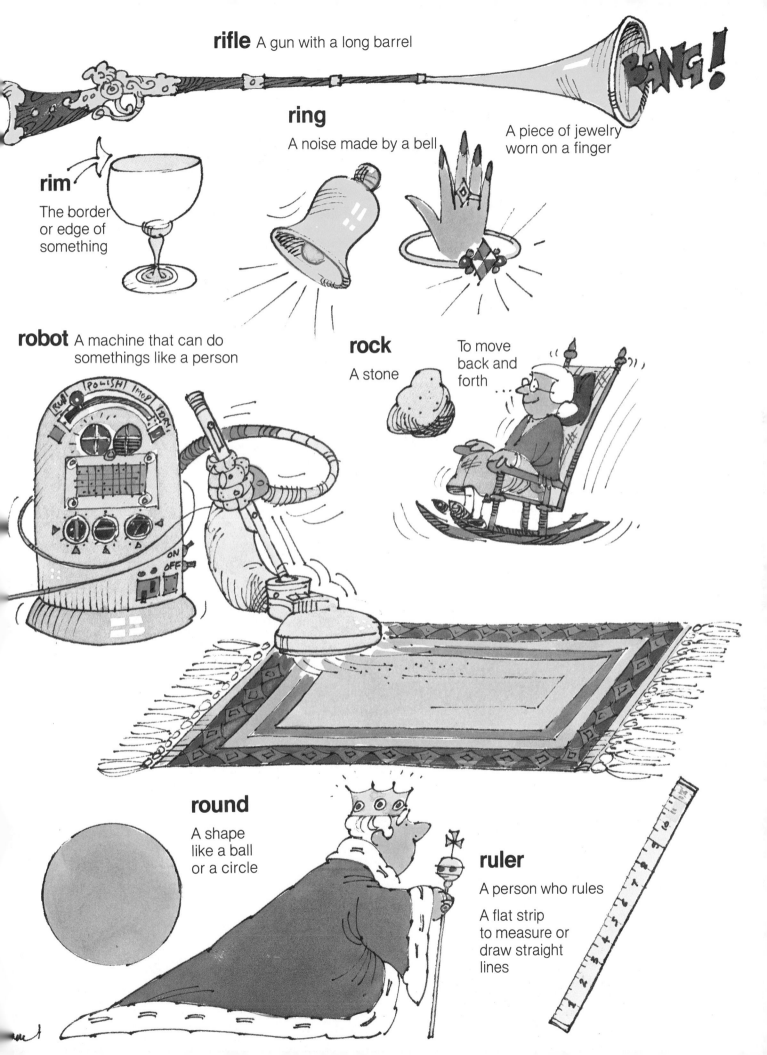

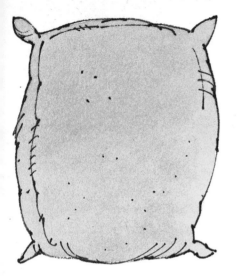

sack A large bag made of strong coarse material

sad Unhappy

saddle A seat for a rider on the back of an animal

salad A cold food made from a combination of vegetables or fruits with other foods

same
Just like something else

sample
A piece or portion of something to show what the whole thing is like

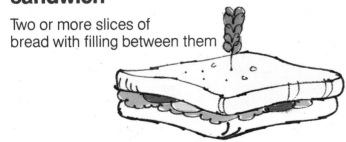

sand Tiny grains of rocks usually found on beaches and deserts

sandwich
Two or more slices of bread with filling between them

saucer
A small dish that is used under a cup

scale
A machine for weighing

Notes of music

scalp
The skin on top of the head usually covered by hair

scholar
A person with a great deal of knowledge

school
A place for teaching and learning

A large group of fish swimming together

scissors
A cutting instrument with 2 sharp blades

scientist
A person who knows a great deal about a particular science

THE ATOM

scream
To emit a loud piercing sound

HELP!

scratch
To scrape or cut a surface

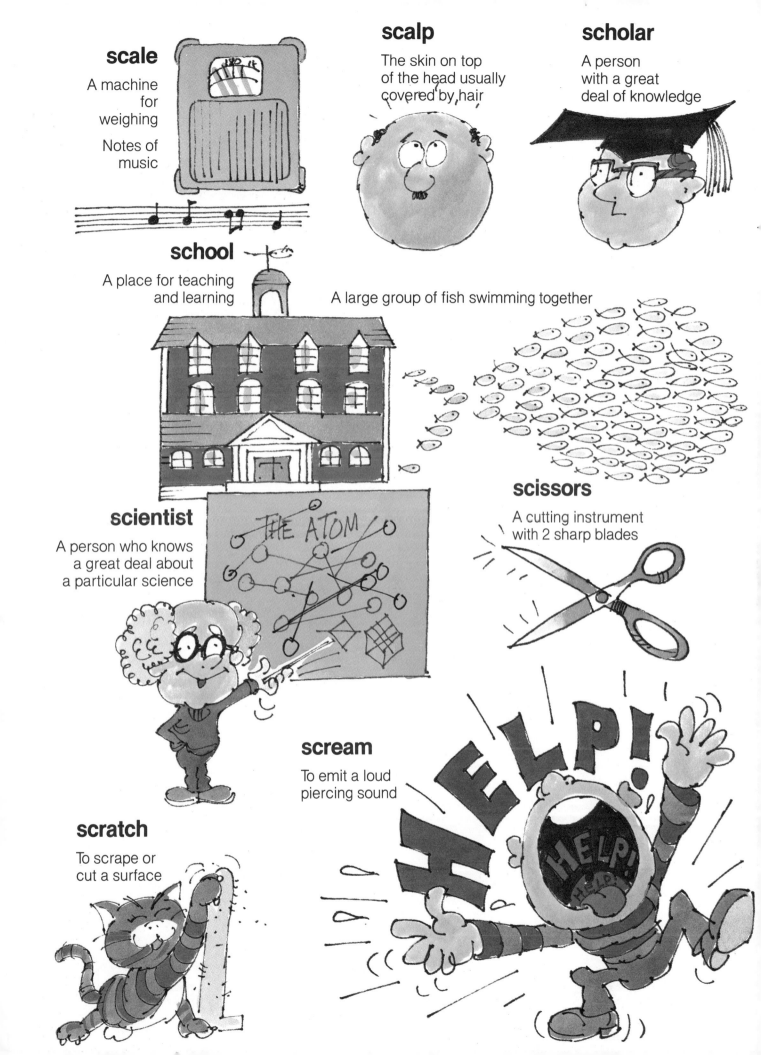

scribble
To write or draw carelessly or with no meaning

sculptor
A person who carves or molds figures or designs

season
One of the four parts of the year

Herbs or spices to add flavor to food

seed
The part of a plant or tree from which a new plant will grow

seek
To search for

CLUE

PUMPKIN

seem
To appear to be

seesaw
An outdoor piece of play equipment for 2 children to go up and down on the ends

several
More than two

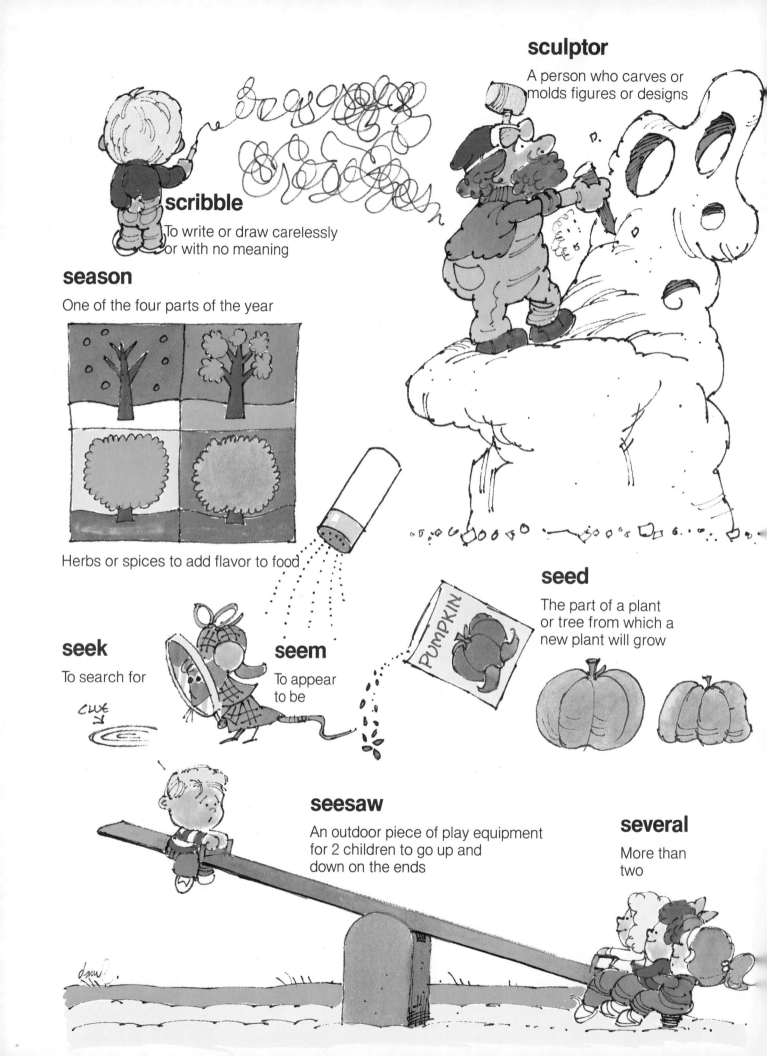

sew
To attach things with stitches

shake
To move up and down or side to side

shampoo
To wash the hair

shape
The form or outline of an object

share To divide something and give to others

shelter
Something to cover or protect

sharp
Having a thin edge that cuts

BE VERY CAREFUL!

DON'T TOUCH!

DANGER! KEEP OFF!

STOP

shin
The front of the leg from the knee to the ankle

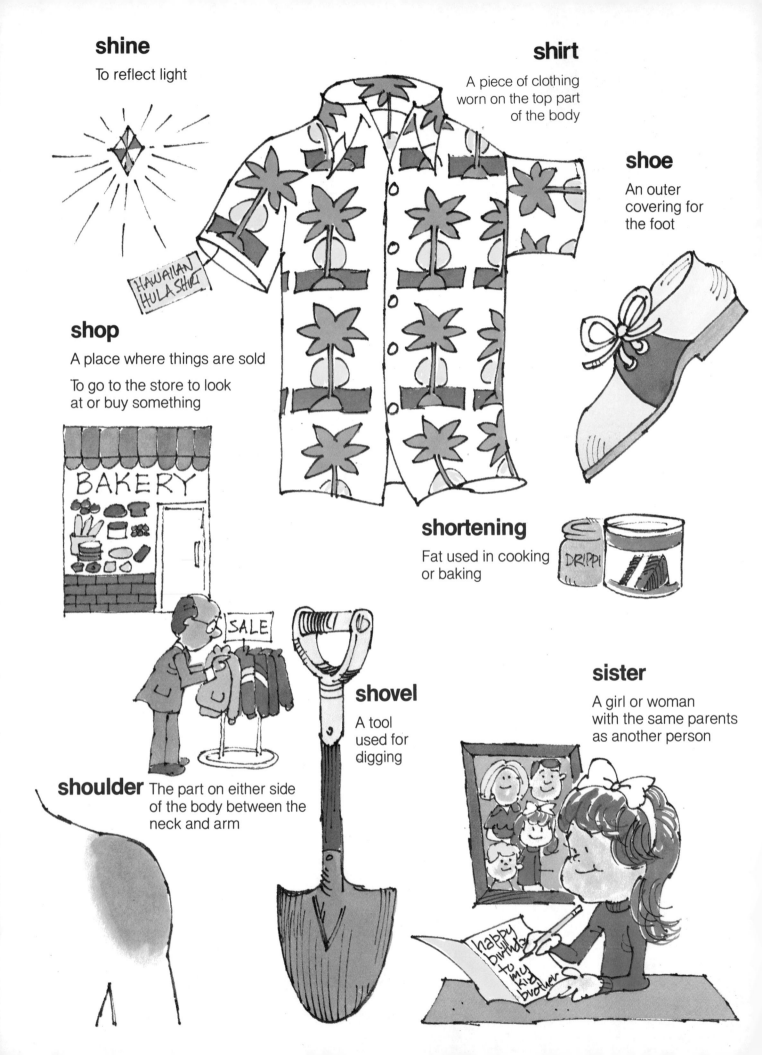

shine

To reflect light

shirt

A piece of clothing worn on the top part of the body

shoe

An outer covering for the foot

shop

A place where things are sold

To go to the store to look at or buy something

shortening

Fat used in cooking or baking

shovel

A tool used for digging

sister

A girl or woman with the same parents as another person

shoulder The part on either side of the body between the neck and arm

sketch

A quick rough drawing

skillet

A shallow pan for frying

skip

To jump over

skin

The outer covering of the body of an animal or person

sleeve

The part of clothing

skirt

The part of a woman's clothing that hangs from the waist down

slacks

Long pants worn by people

slice A piece cut from something larger

slow Not quick

smell

To smell an odor

To have an odor

smile

A happy friendly expression

smooth The surface that is even

sneaker A canvas shoe with rubber soles and laces

son

A male child

sock

A covering for the foot worn under shoes

A punch

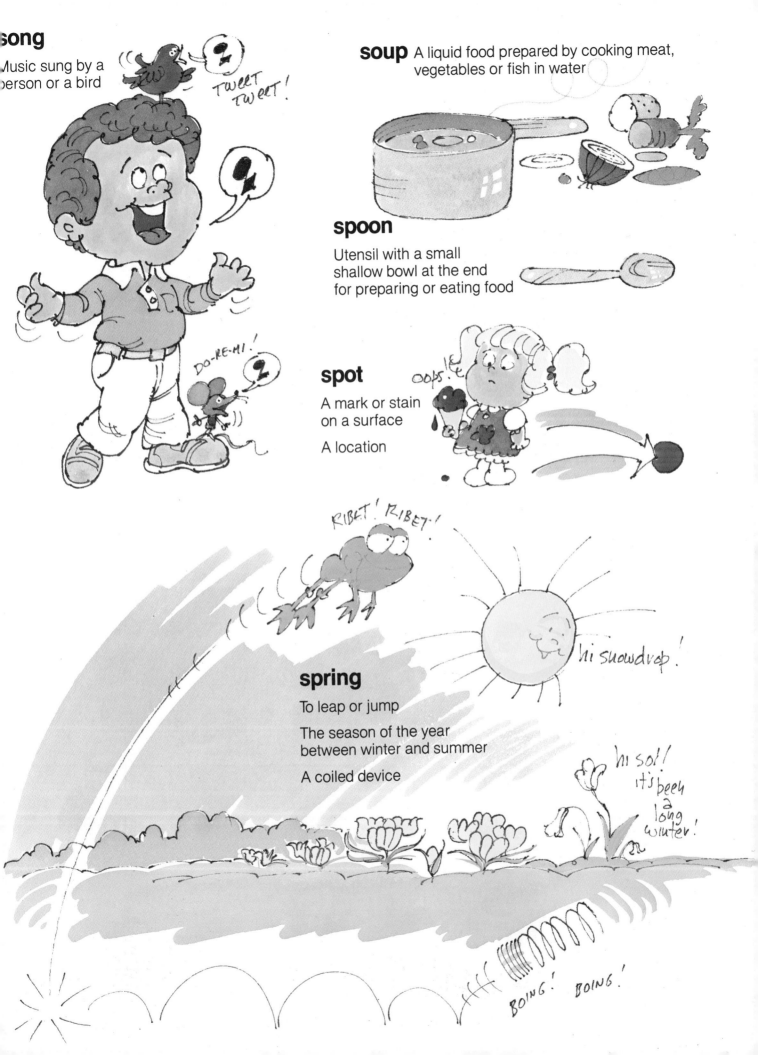

song
Music sung by a
person or a bird

soup
A liquid food prepared by cooking meat,
vegetables or fish in water

spoon
Utensil with a small
shallow bowl at the end
for preparing or eating food

spot
A mark or stain
on a surface

A location

spring
To leap or jump

The season of the year
between winter and summer

A coiled device

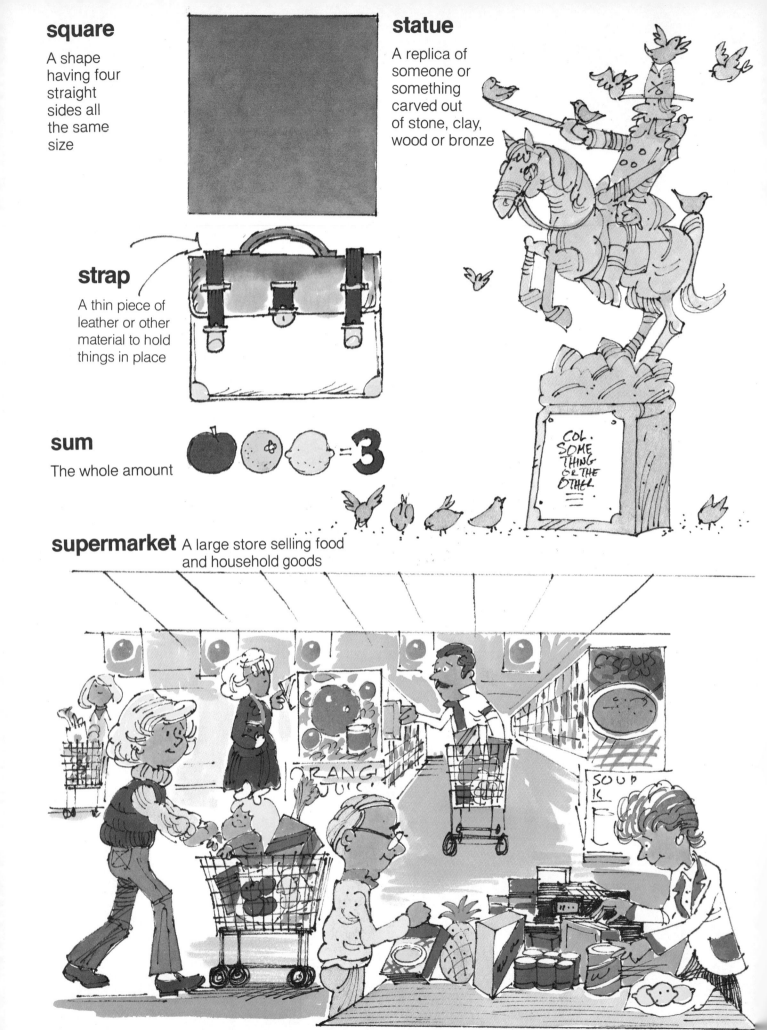

square

A shape having four straight sides all the same size

statue

A replica of someone or something carved out of stone, clay, wood or bronze

strap

A thin piece of leather or other material to hold things in place

sum

The whole amount

supermarket
A large store selling food and household goods

table A piece of furniture with a flat top and legs

tablespoon A large spoon for serving, eating or measuring

tag A label with information that is to something

TO TERRY c/o HIS MOM

TAIL

tail
The part of an animal that sticks out from the back end

tailor
A person who makes repairs or alters clothing

Once upon a time.....

Fairy Tales

tale
A story

tame Gentle, not wild

meow!

puw!

puw

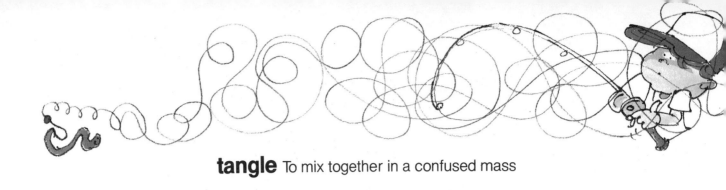

tangle To mix together in a confused mass

task Work that must be done

taste Flavor of food that is taken into the mouth

teach To help someone learn

tease To annoy or bother by making fun of

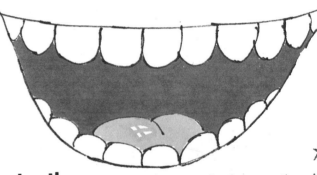

teeth The hard bony parts in the mouth for biting and chewing

telephone An instrument used to send sounds over distances

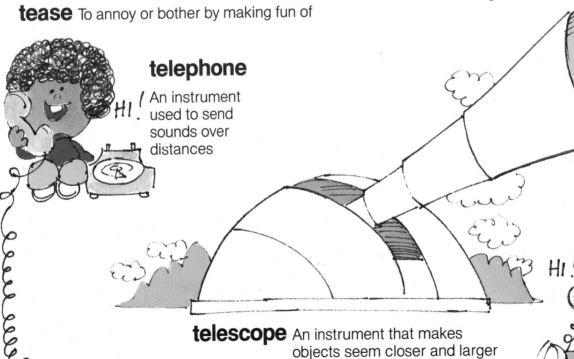

telescope An instrument that makes objects seem closer and larger

television A system for sending and receiving pictures and sound

tenant A person who pays rent to use property owned by another person

tennis

A game in which 2 or 4 people hit a ball over a net with a racket

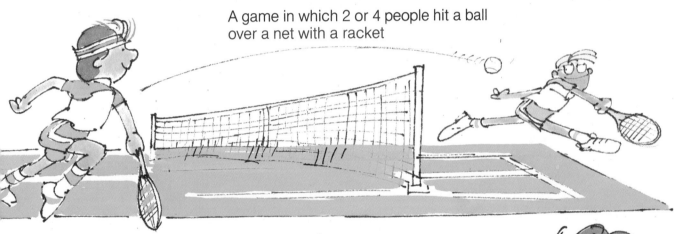

test

A way to find out about the quality of something

thirst

Needing something to drink

thumb

The first finger on the hand

tidy Clean and neat

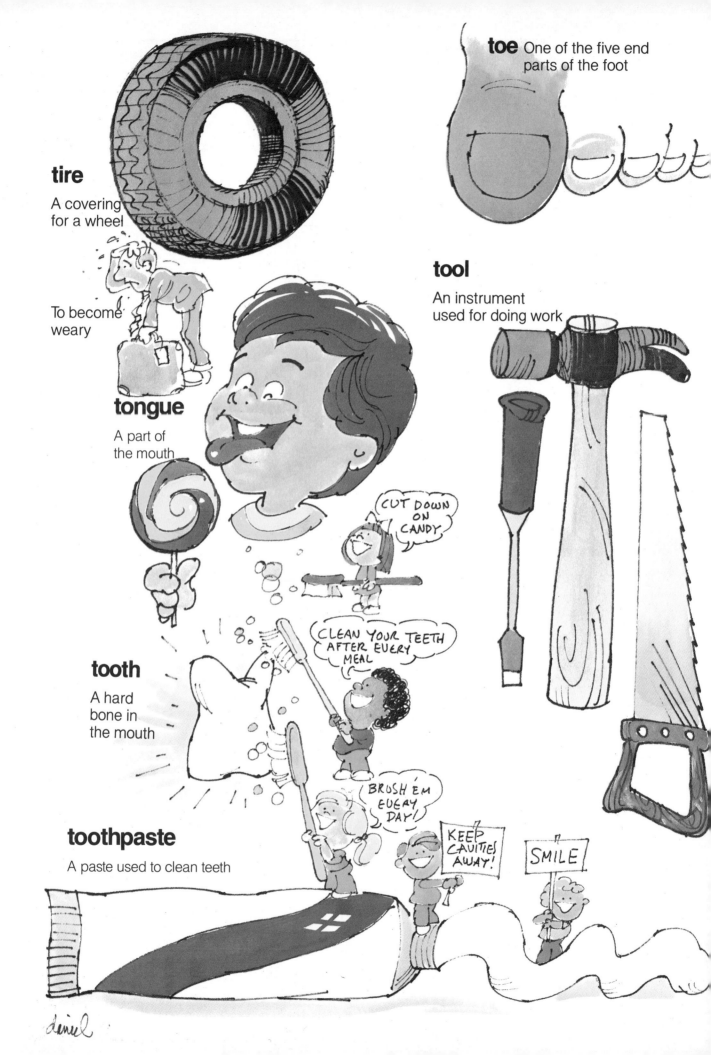

tire

A covering for a wheel

To become weary

tongue

A part of the mouth

tooth

A hard bone in the mouth

toothpaste

A paste used to clean teeth

toe One of the five end parts of the foot

tool

An instrument used for doing work

toss
To throw through the air

toy
A thing a child plays with

trash
Garbage

tray
A flat dish to carry or show things on

tricycle
A vehicle with 3 wheels that can be pedalled

beep! beep!

tripod
A three legged stand to hold a camera or other instrument

umbrella A circular piece of cloth or plastic used to give protection from the rain or sun

uncle The brother of a person's father or mother

umpire A person who rules on plays and actions in certain games and contests

underwear Light clothing worn under outer clothes

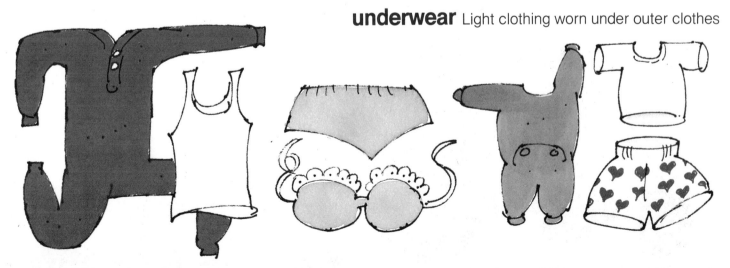

undo
To loosen or unfasten

uneven
Not straight or smooth

unhappy
Not happy

uniform
Special clothing worn by members of a group or organization

universe
The earth, planets and space all together

unkind Mean or not kind

untidy Messy , not tidy

upright

Straight up

upstairs

Up the stairs

unique

The only one
of its kind

utensil

Any tool or device or container
used for making something

vacation
A time or intermission from work used to rest and enjoy

valley The low land between hills or mountains

van A large covered vehicle used for transporting things

vase
A container used to hold flowers or leaves

vat
A large container that can hold liquids

vessel A ship or large boat
A hollow container that can hold liquids

victory

To win a contest

To overcome an enemy

veterinarian

A person who is trained to give
medical care to animals

volume

A collection of
pages or sheets

The quality or
loudness of tone

voyage

A long trip
made on a ship,
plane, aircraft or spacecraft

wagon Vehicle with 4 wheels

waist
The part of the human body between the ribs and the hips

wait To stay in one spot

BUS STOP

waitress
A woman who works in a restaurant

waiter
A man who works in a restaurant

wallet A flat folding case to hold money, cards or photographs

wardrobe
A piece of furniture in which clothes can be kept or hung

waste To use up in a foolish way

PLEASE DEPOSIT YOUR

wash
To make something free of dirt by using soap and water

SOAP

water
Clear, colorless, and tasteless liquid

wave
To signal a greeting by moving the arms and hands

A rolling motion of water in the ocean

weather
The kind of air or atmosphere we live in which can be hot or cold, wet or dry, windy or still

wed
To take a husband or wife

well
A state of being good or healthy

A supply of water coming up from out of the earth

weight
The amount of heaviness of a person or thing

wheel
A round frame that turns and is used on cars or other vehicles

wheelbarrow
A small cart pushed by hand that has a wheel in front and handles in the back

wet
Not dry

whittle To cut off small pieces of wood with a knife

whole Being complete
Having all its parts

wig A covering for the head that looks like hair

wild Living or growing naturally

Not disciplined

window An opening in a wall or ceiling that lets in air or light

wire A thin metal tread

A telegram

RUSH·A·GRAM
CONGRATULATIONS TO THE WINNER!

wink To close and open one eye quickly

woman An adult female person

winner Successful person
Victor in sports

wipe To rub with something in order to clean or dry

wrinkle A small crease or fold on a smooth surface

wrap To cover by folding
A garment used to cover a person usually a cloak or outer garment

wrist The joint between the hand and the arm

write To form characters, letters or words with an instrument on a surface that can then be read

Xmas

Christmas
December 25th

x-ray A special ray that can go through things that regular rays of light cannot do. It is often used by doctors to take pictures of parts inside the body

xylophone

A musical instrument with different sized bars to hit with a mallet to make various notes

yacht A small ship used for pleasure trips

yank A sharp pull

yarn Thread used for weaving or knitting or other crafts

A long adventure story

THEN I PUSHED THE FIRST TIGER OFF MY JEEP...

GEE! WOW! GOSH!

awn o open the mouth ide and take a deep reath

yesterday The day before today

MONDAY DAY SDAY AY SDAY URDAY AY

yo-yo A toy with 2 disks that can spin up and down a string

young Not fully grown

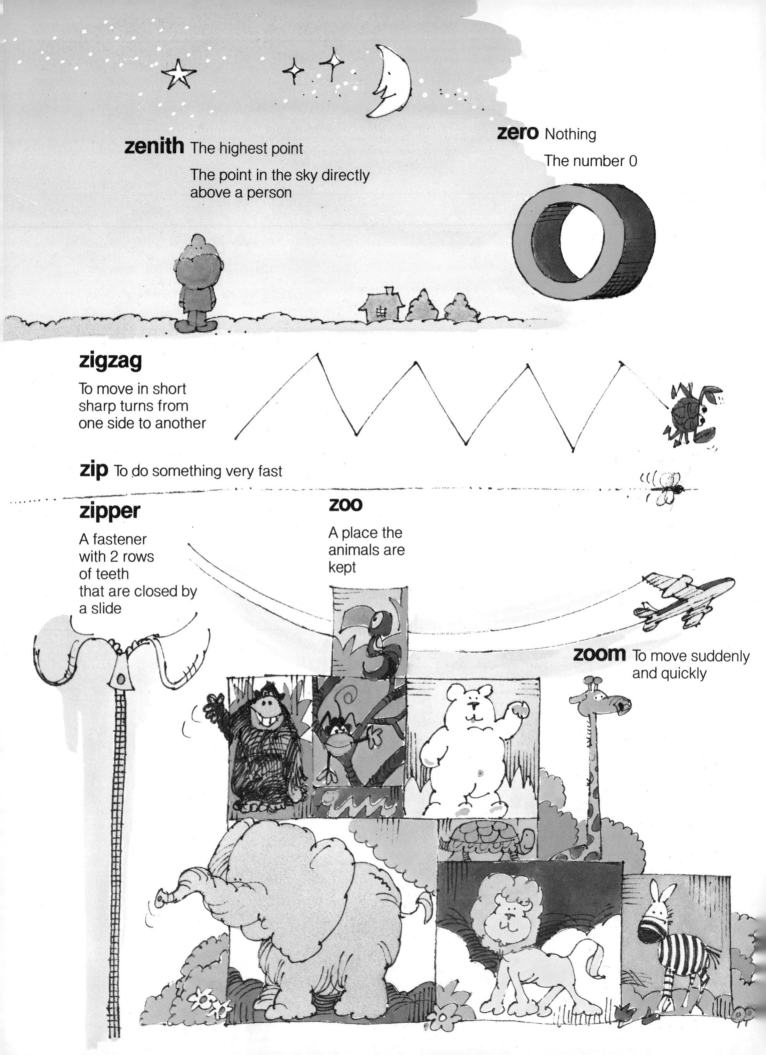

zenith The highest point

The point in the sky directly above a person

zero Nothing

The number 0

zigzag

To move in short sharp turns from one side to another

zip To do something very fast

zipper

A fastener with 2 rows of teeth that are closed by a slide

zoo

A place the animals are kept

zoom To move suddenly and quickly

Aa Bb Cc

Dd Ee Ff

Gg Hh

Ii Jj Kk

Ll Mm